Procrastination Cure

Stop Being Lazy, Get Stuff Done, Master Your Time, Increase Your Productivity And Level Up by Beating Procrastination

Kennedy Felix

Your Free Gift

As a way of thanking you for the purchase, I'd like to offer you a complimentary gift:

- **5 Pillar Life Transformation Checklist:** This short book is about life transformation, presented in bit size pieces for easy implementation. I believe that without such a checklist, you are likely to have a hard time implementing anything in this book and any other thing you set out to do religiously and sticking to it for the long haul. It doesn't matter whether your goals relate to weight loss, relationships, personal finance, investing, personal development, improving communication in your family, your overall health, finances, improving your sex life, resolving issues in your relationship, fighting PMS successfully, investing, running a successful business, traveling etc. With a checklist like this one, you can bet that anything you do will seem a lot easier to implement until the end. Therefore, even if you don't continue reading this book, at least read the one thing that will help you in every other aspect of your life. Grab your copy now by clicking/tapping here or simply enter http://bit.ly/2fantonfreebie into your browser. Your life will never be the same again (if you implement what's in this book), I promise.

PS: I'd like your feedback. If you are happy with this book, please leave a review on Amazon.

Introduction

Victor Kiam, a well-known American entrepreneur and spokesperson for Remington once said,

"Procrastination is opportunity's assassin."

If you are to get better life opportunities, complete your work on time, skyrocket your productivity, and accomplish all your personal and professional goals, you must overcome procrastination. Why? Because if you procrastinate, you will not do anything leave alone do it on time. You will continue to waste the opportunities that come your way.

If you are tired of procrastinating because you've witnessed just how costly procrastination is on your life, this book *will* help you understand why you really procrastinate, what procrastination does to your life and why you must beat it. It then provides workable strategies that will help you get rid of this thief of time, happiness and opportunities for good.

If you are ready to move on to an active, progressive life, this is the book for you.

Table of Contents

Part 1: Understanding Procrastination

Professor Clarry H. Lay, a well-known psychologist and writer, says, *"You procrastinate when there exists a temporal gap between your enacted and intended behavior. When there is a substantial time gap between when you intend to do something and the time at which you actually start working on that task."*

Procrastination happens when you put off things you should be doing right now for later. For instance, if you are supposed to start working on your thesis today but you fail to do it for 2 consecutive weeks, that is procrastination. Usually, you put off completion of those tasks and instead, do something else that you find more enjoyable, relaxing, and comfortable.

Well, the truth is; occasional procrastination is not bad. In fact, at one point or the other, each of us experiences the urge to delay work, do nothing even when we ought to be doing something, and just be lazy. That is alright; we are at liberty to do so and sometimes, doing so is healthy. However, if this practice becomes habitual and you postpone completion of important, high priority, and urgent tasks, procrastination turns into something ugly that has adverse effects on your life.

The Real Reasons Why We Procrastinate

When you are postponing a task, you give yourself all kinds of reasons – most of them are simply excuses. Our reasons are never true; we just make them up and make them so convincing that we and everybody else believes them. You may say you are tired, you do not have the time, you are not in the right frame of mind, and you do not have the necessary resources and so on. When you look deeper and you are true to yourself, none of these 'blocks' are as definite as you make them appear. There is always something you can do to get around them. They are not the real reasons why you procrastinate.

Here are the real culprits:

1: *We avoid pain*

We refuse to take action because it involves a certain amount pain. To ascertain if this is true, do the following;

Close your eyes and take slow and deep breaths until you are calm. Think about the action you have been avoiding. It could be something like updating your resume or completing your thesis. Imagine yourself beginning to take action, for instance doing the necessary research to get content for the thesis. How does it feel? You are probably feeling something unpleasant. Concentrate on that feeling.

Whatever you choose to call it maybe fear, vulnerability, anxiety, stress and so on; these are feelings that no one likes and they all are forms of pain.

Everybody wants to avoid pain but sometimes we can only move forward if we choose to face it and go through it. However, not everyone wants to acknowledge this fact – most would rather keep running. This is why there are so many chronic procrastinators.

2: We hold our comfort zones dear

Some of us postpone tasks for the love of our comfort zones. To achieve things we know we should is not easy and most times, we must leave our comfort zones. The thing is; productivity requires that you go an extra mile and in a comfort zone, there is no extra mile – it consists of everything you are used to and comfortable with.

Without being aware of it, most of us, when confronted with a situation we are not familiar with or that, which requires a little more effort, we retreat to our comfort zones. Because of fear of the unfamiliar, we try our best never to leave our so beloved zones. For instance, a person who shies away from public speaking may avoid any event where they are required to interact with unfamiliar people, even an interview for a promising job.

3: Poor time management

If you do not plan your time well, you do not expect everything to be done when it's supposed to be. You won't help but to let tasks spill over to the next hour or day when you are supposed to be doing something else. This way, tasks end up being displaced and pushed forward until sometimes they are not done at all.

For instance, you plan to review an essay for school at 5 am before you start preparing for work at 6 am to get there at 7 am so you can browse through some information to reply to a clients query by 8 am. However, you snooze your 4:30 am alarm and end up waking up at 5:30am. Your professor needs that essay reviewed and submitted and so you begin your review at 5:45 am. You decide that you can leave the house at 7:45 promising yourself that there will be no traffic then. Just like that, everything gets pushed and needless to say, the tasks for the day will not be accomplished.

4: The thirst for instant gratification

The need to feel good right now – it is a big problem in the 21st century. In this century we are living in, people have forgotten to save the best for last. We want to do things that make us happy now and keep pushing the less pleasant forward. For instance, instead of washing dishes and then enjoying a movie later, a person wants to watch a movie and do the dishes later. They want to relax but after doing nothing. It is likely that such a person will end up binging on movies till late and there will be no time or energy left to do dishes. But they can be done tomorrow, right? That's how the cycle continues.

5: *Fear of failure or accomplishment*

When you do not want your capabilities judged, you are most likely to avoid doing work. You do not want to look stupid, to do poorly or do too well. You do not want anyone or even yourself knowing what you are capable of because you are afraid of being challenged or criticized for your failure or accomplishment. Also, if you are afraid that you might do poorly, procrastinating will give you the excuse of 'not having enough time to do it well'.

When you procrastinate all the time, you can be sure to experience a wide array of negative effects. Let's discuss that.

The Dark Side of Procrastination: How Procrastination Affects Your Life

We are all guilty of procrastination at some point in our day to day activities. However, there are those who are lucky enough to catch the vice in time and put it under control. There are yet the unlucky or ignorant ones who allow it space in their lives.

If you entertain procrastination in your life, it will wreck it. Here's is how it will destroy you:

1. You Lose Time

A common quote states that 'procrastination is the thief of time'. Also, Benjamin Franklin once said,

"You may delay, but time will not."

This quote highlights just how precious time is; it also illuminates why you must not procrastinate because if you do, you will lose this precious and non-renewable resource. Procrastinators squander the most precious asset gifted to man. They live as if they have all the time in the world and are blind to the fact that as human beings, our time on earth is limited. Every moment is an opportunity we shall never have again.

And the worst thing about procrastination in relation to time is, no matter your reasons, time will never understand and thus it will never delay or stop to wait for you. Like Mr.

Franklin observed, time is always on the move, with or without you. One day, five years later, you will look back to find that you are still the same. You did not use the time to improve yourself and you will wonder, 'where did all the time go?' Well, your procrastinating habit stole it. What did it leave you with? The helpless feeling of regret since you cannot turn back the hands of time.

2: Work Keeps Pilling Up

Naturally, when you never complete your tasks and you squander the time when they are supposed to be done, you will miss many deadlines. Not doing tasks does not make them disappear. At the end of the day, they will be right there waiting for you and thus your work will continue piling. Before you realize it, your work will be an inescapable tsunami.

3: You Miss Out On Good Opportunities

Imagine you were supposed to renew your visa two weeks ago but you put it off because you would rather go out with your friends on that free day. Your company now needs to send someone overseas and they chose you. However, you cannot go because your visa is expired! Let's look at another real life example:

You go to a social event and see a person you have wanted to talk to for a while, may be a possible soul mate. You do not go to them immediately; rather, you put it off for when you are ready or at the end of the party when there aren't many people around. Unfortunately, when you feel ready to talk, you see them with someone else or they have already left. You may have just missed your life partner!

Procrastination will make you miss out on life changing opportunities. As they say, opportunities when missed may never reoccur. Someone else who is more prepared will grab them and you will only remain miserable.

4: You Fail to Fulfill any of Your Goals

You will set goals but procrastination will help you smash them, ever time. Remember; goals have a timeline. If you keep pushing them, when will you ever get to achieve them within the set time? The answer is, NEVER.

As a procrastinator, your goals will always be on the back burner. As you set them, they seem to be important; they are a priority. However, dreaming and setting goals are one thing but getting to work to achieve them is the main challenge. As a procrastinator, getting to work especially if you are required to put in a lot of effort will be a struggle as you prefer the more pleasant options. What do you become? A person who dreams big but never achieves a thing – a no good loser.

5: You Lose Value For Yourself

It begins when you never do anything that you say you will do. You are also missing out on opportunities that you know would change your life not because you are incapable but because you are just lazy. You know that you can never rely on yourself because you will always let yourself down. You begin to hate yourself.

When this happens, you have lost your sense of self-worth. Your self-esteem is on the floor and a once confident person becomes a sad, withdrawn and bitter individual. They have lost value for themselves and life has lost meaning, which is one of the worst things that can happen to a human being.

6: You Lose Credibility- No One Trusts You Anymore

What happens when you keep telling people that you will do things but you never actually get them done? For instance, you promise your spouse that you will get the kitchen sink fixed over the weekend. Weeks pass by and it's always an excuse why you never got it done. Soon, they will stop believing in you; your word will mean nothing to them anymore. They will eventually get someone else to do it.

Trust is not easy to build but it is incredibly easy to destroy. It's terrible when the people around you never believe or trust in you to get the simplest things done. Sadly, when you lose credibility with people, it is very hard to restore it. Now, when there is no trust, relationships with family, friends and even colleagues suffer.

7: **Your Health Suffers**

Procrastination puts your health at risk. You may ask how. Let me explain it to you:

In the beginning of the year, almost everybody makes the famous New Year resolutions concerning their health. You ate too much during the holidays and your first goal is to lose the weight you gained, detox, develop an exercise routine and cultivate healthy eating habits. This is your first goal but only on paper. You set these goals but you keep delaying to start on them. Six months later, you are getting unhealthier and the pounds have piled on.

It's not only about New Year health resolutions but most of the resolves concerning our health require a lot of change and shifting from the feel good zones. No wonder we procrastinate on them so much and our health keeps deteriorating.

Stress and anxiety

These have been named as silent killers and procrastination is a major trigger. When you have not achieved your goals, you have not beat deadlines and when you know there is some pending work that you have been avoiding, you will get anxious and most likely end up stressed or worse depressed. These will have a negative effect on your body leading to development of other health issues. Research by Psychology Today shows that compared to those complete their work on time, those who procrastinate often suffer from insomnia, colds, flu and gastrointestinal issues.

8. It Will Steal Your Happiness

You put important things off so you can concentrate on the pleasant stuff first. However, they will not give you lasting satisfaction. There in the back of your mind will be a constant reminder that you ought to be doing something else. For this reason, you will not be completely happy.

Secondly, as we have seen earlier, a procrastinator loses value for themselves and credibility with others. Deep inside, even though they may pretend on the outside, they feel worthless. Their loved ones cannot count on them much. There is a void that can only be filled by self love and love and appreciation by others. With ruined relationships with self and others, a procrastinator cannot be happy with themselves or with others.

9. It Could Ruin Your Career

Your productivity drops when you never get stuff done on time. For instance, it drops when you have an important task to complete at work but since its challenging, you lose concentration and check your Facebook feed every 10 minutes. At the end of the day, you spend 80% of your time on social media and 20% on work. You cannot work this way and be a productive employee. You will not meet/achieve deadlines this way. What consequences will this have on your career?

An unproductive employee will have poor performance, which is not rewarded. For this reason, you miss out on pay raises and promotions. If you continue slacking, you will eventually not be worth keeping – you lose your job.

There is nothing good about procrastinating. You do not want to have it blow the good things away from you. You need to live the life you want and you cannot let this monster take it away from you. If you have been struggling to stop procrastinating for a while but you just could not beat the habit, here is new hope for you. The next part of this book will teach you how to beat procrastination for good.

Part 2: How To Beat Procrastination

There is no one single way to beat procrastination. As we have discussed earlier, it originates from the mind and is linked to complex psychological reasons. This indicates just how deep it is rooted. If you are to get rid of it, you have to dig it up from the roots. The process involves a number of steps that will be discussed below:

Step 1: Awareness and Acknowledgement

If you want to solve a problem, the first step is to understand its root; reasons why. Without this understanding, you cannot come up with an effective solution. As with other problems, the key to figuring out how to conquer the procrastination habit is awareness and acknowledgment. You have to be aware that the problem exists, acknowledge that you are suffering from it and know the purpose it serves in your life. Here's how to do that:

Find Out If You Are A Procrastinator

Track your time

Every one of us under the sun has 24 hour days. How do you spend yours? How many hours do you spend doing constructive things and being productive and how many do you spend doing other unhelpful stuff?

Most of us can say that we are busy all day. Unfortunately, we interpret busyness for productiveness. Have you ever stopped to analyze how you spend your time and what exactly you are doing when you are busy? For instance, when you report to work at 8 am and you are supposed to close your working day at 5 pm, can you say that you spend all those hours working on important tasks as you are required to? How many times have you paused work for two hours or more to shop, check social media, day dream or chat with colleagues?

To identify if you are a procrastinator hiding in 'busyness', you have to keep a log to track how you spend your time and how much time you spend on tasks.

What to do

Create a spreadsheet that has the following columns: **Task, Starting Time**, **Ending Time**, **Total Time Spent on Task**, and **Task Finished/Work in Progress/Postponed.** Also, have a place for **Comments** to record explanations for why a task is postponed or record interruptions.

To track the time you commit to the tasks you are supposed to be working on, whenever you start a task, record it in that spreadsheet, logging it under *'starting time'*. Whenever you complete the task, record the exact time you finish it under *'completion time'*. Calculate the time spent doing the task by subtracting the completion time from the starting time and record it under *Total time spent on task*. If the task had a deadline, this time should be recorded under *'completion time'*. If the task is not finished past this time, tick the *postponed* column. If it is finished, tick the *'task completed'* column. Do this for at least 10 days. After the 10 days, go through the spreadsheet and analyze how you performed. Did tasks get completed in time? Did you spend more much time than necessary on tasks often? Was there a lot of postponing?

If your record shows any of the following, you are a habitual procrastinator:

- Reading your emails first thing in the morning and taking too much time going through them without working on any substantial task,

- Tackling low priority tasks first and spending quite a substantial amount of time on them. A low priority task is any task that does not contribute much to your productivity or the fulfillment of your goals.

- Jumping from one task to another, without completely getting finished with one first.

- Napping, watching movies/television, browsing the web, or using your phone after 10 minutes of working on a task.

- Sitting down to do a high priority task and putting it on pause to do something else that 'just came up'.

- Not starting a task on time, especially for tasks that have a deadline where you end up spending less time than required on a task.

- Putting a task on hold as a work in progress to waiting for the perfect time, mood, circumstances or method to work on a task especially a high priority one.

- Using the 'task is too difficult' statement as an excuse to postpone high priority tasks.

- Doing nothing at the start of the day and ending your day with a few unimportant tasks. You can track this time by checking when you start tasks on a particular day.

If your observations and records show a recurrent occurrence of any 2 to 3 of these signs, you are a procrastinator. Now that you know that you are a victim of this problem, what kind of victim are you?

Identify the Kind of Procrastinator You Are

Not all procrastinators are the same. They are made different by their triggers – which differ. Identifying the kind of procrastination you practice is essential in helping you uproot the practice for good. Now let's find out what you are in the procrastinator's world:

The ostrich

They say that the ostrich likes to bury its head in the sand. This could be interpreted that this bird likes to hide from the realities surrounding it – it prefers to stay in the dream stage of things. They love the dream world because they do not have to work for real or face things like stress, criticism or hardship.

The ostrich procrastinator has big visions and ambitious plans, but which only exist in their dream. It is sad that dreaming about this great things gives them a false sense of achievement such that they never get up to do any work. Their big dreams never see the light of day.

The perfectionist

This procrastinator derives pleasure from being perfect. For this reason, they would never dare to show any imperfection. They are forever looking for the perfect conditions; timing, approach, information. Lack of them becomes the excuse why they never complete tasks. Instead of working within the available conditions to finish a task, the perfectionist is caught up in excuses and a never ending cycle of edits, additions and deletions.

The chicken

This type of procrastinator does not put any effort to think their actions through. They do not prioritize their work; rather, they do what they feel they should do – and not what they need to do.

A chicken thinks that the extra time needed to plan for and prioritize tasks is a wasted thus they would rather just jump into action, tackling random tasks. This is why they will spend a lot of time tackling effortless tasks that do not contribute much to a project while ignoring the high impact tasks.

The daredevil

This kind of procrastinator claims that they work best under pressure that they believe that close deadlines will push them to do better. Instead of having a schedule to complete tasks, they would rather enjoy the time doing things that give them pleasure before the deadline draws near.

The daredevils have managed to get away by doing work hurriedly in the last minute, which has caused them to believe that there is no use to start early and sacrifice their pleasure time. Often, because of rushing their work, they compromise its quality.

The self – saboteur

This person is afraid of making mistakes or doing anything wrong. They will not take time to learn or put any effort to do a task right. They believe that the only way they can avoid making mistakes is by doing nothing at all. They have a common belief; 'by doing nothing, bad things will not happen'. Ultimately, they make few mistakes but also they see few achievements too.

Having known the kind of procrastination you experience, the next step is to find ways to overcome it. The trigger determines the steps you take to overcome it. The next steps involve finding ways to eliminate the procrastination triggers so you can be set free.

Step 2: Change Your Mindset

The mind is where habits are bred. Procrastination, as we have discussed earlier, is a habit that is purely bred in the mind. The most definite way to conquer it is to uproot it from the roots; you have to change your mindset from that which encourages this vice to one that encourages productive habits.

When we talk of a mindset, we are referring to the ideologies, beliefs and thoughts that you nurture in the mind. These things determine your actions and who you become. Whatever issues you have, they stem from your mindset. This is why when you change it, you change your world. We are going to discuss mindset shifts you need to make so you can beat procrastination and achieve your full potential. This step applies to all procrastination triggers.

1: Develop A Growth Mindset

A major reason why we put off tasks is fear. We are afraid to fail, to be criticized and to look stupid. For this reason, we seek to be perfect and when we suspect that we might not have the information or know how required, we shy away from tasks. This happens because we have a fixed mindset.

The nature of a fixed mindset

In a fixed mindset, one believes that knowledge, intelligence or talent is a fixed trait that a person is born with. They believe that people who are good at something or those who succeed were born to be successful – because of a natural ability. For this reason, if they do not succeed, they will give an excuse that it's not in them. They do not believe in effort; they think it's a waste of time

Also, individuals with a fixed mindset seek to validate themselves. Any failure is humiliating because they are more concerned about the opinion of others rather than learning from their failures. This is why they will avoid any task that they suspect they may not excel in.

With a fixed mindset, any new challenge is a no-no. You avoid it like a plague because you cannot stand being judged. If you are engaged in task and new obstacles arise, you are likely to give up quickly and watch Netflix instead.

The fixed mindset is a very harmful one to hold. You do not give yourself a chance to develop your potential. You will always live less than you are capable of and never improve. This kind of mindset keeps procrastination thriving.

Ditch the fixed mindset for a growth mindset

In a growth mindset, you hold the belief that you can develop any ability through hard work and commitment. This belief gives you the desire to try new things and to learn. You are more receptive of challenges and you do not shy away from setbacks.

This kind of mindset helps you appreciate and embrace effort. You will commit yourself fully while employing all the effort you can muster to get a task done. Failure is not something you avoid, because your focus is not about validating yourself but rather on developing your skill – you know that failure is a part of the learning process. Ultimately, the growth mindset leads you to an up-ward path of continued development, reaching higher levels of mastery in any field and greater productivity.

How To Change Your Mindset

The fixed mindset is common with procrastinators. If you want to get rid of the procrastination problem, employ the following steps to shift to the growth mindset.

Step 1: Beware of your fixed mindset 'voice'

This is the voice of the 'inner saboteur' inside your head. It is the voice that undermines your effort and criticizes your work. In the face of a new challenge, you may hear, "Are you really sure you can handle it?" "What if you flop?"

When you are faced with obstacles, it reminds you how incapable you are. It may whisper, "I told you that you didn't have it in you" or "If only you were talented"

Once you know that you have a fixed mindset and you anticipate to hear these voices, you are less likely to believe them. You can always retort, "I knew you would say that."

Step 2: Understand that the fixed mindset voice stems from fear

You heard that voice but it is important that you know that there is no truth in what it says. It is just speaking from fear. It could be a fear of being judged, a few of failure, criticism and so on.

Step 3: Embrace the fear

You feel the fear; I know it is scary but you should not run from it. Did you know that an unacknowledged fear is a fuel for the fixed mindset? You can only win over this mindset if you stay and face the fear. It is nothing more than just an emotion so welcome it and stay present within it. Eventually, it will not be strong enough to hold you – it will disappear and stop dominating your behavior.

Step 4: Recognize that you have the freedom to make a choice

Once you hear the sabotaging voice, you have two options; you can choose to listen and believe what they say about your lack of ability and talent or you can view this as a sign that you should start challenging yourself then step up your effort and change your strategies.

Do not let the voices put you down. No matter what they say, make a conscious choice to let the voice challenge you to do better and to develop. Strive to prove them wrong.

Step 5: Talk back to the saboteur with a growth mindset

When the fixed mindset says, 'what if you fail", the growth mindset voice answers, " failure is part of the learning process" or " most successful people I know failed terribly at first".

Whenever you face difficulty and the fixed mindset voice says, "if only you had talent, you would ace this" Let the growth mindset voice retort, "Even Mohammed Ali was not born a natural boxer. He had to put on tons of effort to become the best."

You could write out these dialogues in a journal; it will be easier for you to connect to these voices when you write what they say. Also, it's a good record which you can review later. You could always list the winning voice in every dialogue – let the winner be the growth mindset voice.

Step 6: Take action, guided by the growth mindset voice

In step 5, you responded to the saboteur with the growth mindset voice. In this final step, you ought to determine how you will take the necessary action – determine a course of action that will lead to growth. It may include taking on new challenges, persistence in the face of difficulty or adjusting your effort to match challenges.

Adding to the 6 steps, here are questions that can help you lean towards a growth mindset instead of running from or delaying tasks:

1. What steps can I take to help me succeed in this task?

2. Am I aware of the outcome I am after?

3. When/where/how will I follow through with my plan?

4. Where can I get the information needed?

5. Is my current strategy working? If not, how can I improve it?

6. What mistake did I make? Did I learn anything from it?

2: Adopting A Positive Mindset – Positive Thinking

Procrastination is a form of negative thinking – the opposite of positive thinking. Negative thoughts focus on the dark side of things. They show you how impossible a task is, how incapable you are, how it's not a good time to start and so on. When you give in to these negative thoughts, you give in to inaction. You convince yourself that you will act when the conditions are better – which they may never get.

The best tool to battle procrastination is developing the kind of thinking that counters the one it thrives in; Develop positive thinking. It helps you look at the bright side of things which inspires action. If you see possibilities in the midst of impossibility, you will find a way to maneuver through conditions even when they are not favorable or find a way to make them work for you. There is a way you can tune your negative thinking brain to start thinking positively.

1: Reframe your mental models

Where do negative thoughts/beliefs come from? They form because of our mental models. The formation of a mental model directly correlates with your past experiences. It is based upon your perception of your surroundings and how things work – according to your past experiences.

When these perceptions and thoughts planted in your mind, they will determine your behavior, reaction and approaches to specific tasks. If you currently hold negative perceptions about a task, it is likely that your reasoning and decision making skills will be diverted to procrastination – because you do not expect a positive outcome.

Mental models are not easy to break; you cannot just overcome them by deciding to change your thinking. A mental model is made of three parts which create a strong bond – you need to break the three to break the bond. For instance, a destructive mental model includes a negative thought, a mental picture and a negative emotion. To overcome it, you not only have to reverse negative thoughts but also you have to replace the negative emotion with a positive one and attach it to the mental picture. Look at the following example.

You have a task that you are required to explain a certain process, say combustion. It is a project that will require you to do a lot of research. You may have done this before and you may have disliked going through pages and pages of information, sometimes not getting what you are looking for. Every time you hear that you have to do research on something, you picture those pages and you get a negative emotion like boredom. And so you automatically respond with procrastination. You will unconsciously respond that way because of the mental model you developed towards research. To stop procrastinating on such tasks, you will need to develop a new mental model;

First, change your thoughts about research. Think of it as something that exposes you to a lot of material that provides you with useful knowledge that can be used in the future. View the pages and pages of information that you have to go through as a rare opportunity to learn.

Once you form the new belief, to see it as something that you like, you will be approaching the tasks that used to bore you out of your mind in a new positive light. This positivity triggers a positive reaction in the mind and you will find that instead of dreading the task, the brain is stimulated to get into action to find the nuggets of wisdom – even if you will not find the information you are looking for. So when you hear research, you picture the many pages you will read, you will get a positive emotion like good curiosity that will drive you to get started.

2: Teach yourself to be grateful always

Life is not fair; it will not always hand you the best things. However, though it is not an easy attitude to keep, try to be grateful even when things are not as good as you want them to be. Sometimes, one single negative event can ruin your day. The mind tends to cling to negativity and that's how you find a 5 minute negative event stealing 24 hours that you will spend doing nothing other than fuss and be angry. Remember this time could be spent on doing something worthwhile, which you of course put off until you feel better.

However, you could intentionally focus on the good parts of everything. When they give a task that is too tough, see that they are giving you an opportunity to grow your mind and abilities. When you lose an important research, take it as an opportunity to work hard again to come up with an even better one. When you are grateful, you make it hard for destructive negative emotions to creep inside your mind thus you are able to maintain focus on the important tasks ahead.

3: Change your perception of challenges

A Best Selling author, Robert Kiyosaki has this to say about challenges; *"sometimes you win, sometimes you learn"*. The problem with most of us is we want to win always. Mr. Kiyosaki believes that there are no dead ends in life; there is nothing like failure or losing. When you do not win, you have an opportunity to learn.

View challenges as opportunities to stretch. Have fun with them as if they were adventures. Sometimes they may overpower you, not because you did not try hard but because of circumstances beyond your control. Understand that you cannot control everything but you can control your effort. When you fail, increase your effort and if you fail again, there should be no regret so long as you gave it your all. Next time try harder. The more the tries, the more the experience gained.

4: See obligations as privileges

Most of us label things as obligations unnecessarily. For instance, when you say, I have to go to work, I have to finish this task, I have to complete this book and so on, you are telling your brain that it has to do those things or else. These will most likely result into negative emotions like dread and that's how you find yourself hating tasks and procrastinating.

Replace the word 'have' with 'get'. When you say I get to go to work, I get to finish this book and so on, you make it sound like you are privileged to be doing those tasks – it is a way of showing gratitude. Remember, there is someone who does not have work to go to and another who cannot afford to write a book but you have the privilege to have these tasks. When you change from seeing things you have to do to appreciating things you get to do, you will have a more positive approach on tasks and be happier and less stressed.

5: Point out problems – but come up with solutions

Thinking positively does not mean that you become oblivious to problems. It means that you get to criticize but with an intention to make things better – it is called constructive criticism. Point out problems in people, tasks or situations. If something is wrong, do not be afraid to mention it. However, instead of pointing out problems and sitting on the sidelines complaining (which is a waste of time), put in effort to find solutions to make it better.

6: Desist from getting dragged into other people's complaints

Negativity is strong and has a way of pulling as many culprits as it can. Have you ever gone to work, psyched about the day and then when you are about to start working, a co-worker starts complaining about the boss or how they are being overworked? You had not thought like that before, but now that they mentioned it, you start seeing ways in which you have been mistreated, how your skills are being misused and so on. Before you know it, you have joined the complaint-fest. As a result, your psyche is gone, negativity about your job sets in and every task is a bother.

To keep sane and positive and to maintain your productivity, do not allow yourself to be pulled into people's complaints. If they won't stop even when asked to, walk away if you have to and never ever contribute to such conversations. If you participate, you not only ruin that day but every other day the complainer is around. Why? Your participation gives them validation, which encourages them to find more problems to complain about every day. If you don't pay any attention, they will complain less and you can have your peace.

7: Take a breathe

Have you noticed how anxiety, stress or fear makes us change the normal way we breathe? Breathe is directly connected to our emotions and thus it changes depending on our feelings. The good thing about this is that you can use this connection to change how you feel – you can change your feelings by changing how you breathe!

This is to say that whenever you feel overwhelmed by something, say a challenging task and you feel negative emotions like stress or anxiety setting in; all you may need to do is to just breathe. These emotions tend to make you breathe fast. You could step away from the task and counter them by taking deep slow breathes. You will be surprised at how calm you become and then you can be able to reset your mind and begin again.

Step 3: Change The Way You Think And Feel About Work And Procrastination

What are your thoughts about your work; how do you feel when you know that there is a task you are supposed to work on? Do you want to work on it or would you rather pass it off and do something else?

Many times, we struggle with motivation to get started on a task and the urge to procrastinate. Several reasons which are connected to the nature of the brain can explain this:

- This may be as a result of the risk-reward calculation about your ability to succeed that your brain is making. This is your ego trying to protect you, especially when you are afraid or uncertain.

- Secondly, our brains lead us to delay tasks, especially those which promise future gratification; it is a natural human trait to value immediate rewards (instant gratification) over future rewards.

- When you cannot mentally comprehend why you need to do a certain task and your focus would rather be somewhere else where the pleasure center of the brain gets satisfied. You see, a procrastinator is likely to nurture a negative mindset about work and feel good thinking about putting it off to do other things that excite them. Addiction to the feel good practices while ignoring the hard and boring tasks is the reason why they turn that one-time practice of delaying a task may be to rest, into a difficult-to-let-go-off habit.

To break this habit for good, you need to start to manipulate your thoughts about work and procrastination. Doing so will help you start thinking and feeling differently such that you focus more on getting things done.

Here is how you can do that.

1: Find Out Why You Nurture a Positive Mindset about Procrastination

Figure out why you feel good postponing your task and what makes you do it again and again. Ask yourself the following questions and make sure you answer them as honestly as you possibly can;

- Do you procrastinate because you find your work too difficult to complete or do you do so because you lack the skill required to complete the task effectively?

- Do you procrastinate because you are not interested in carrying out certain responsibilities, or because you are fearful of not being perfect or failing?

- Do you procrastinate because you tire easily, which is why you prefer relaxing or doing nothing substantial?

Spend time with yourself and ponder upon these questions until you figure out why you enjoy or prefer procrastinating. You can have different reasons for postponing different tasks.

Write down whatever answers you identify and then move to the next step.

2: Make An Evaluation To Determine Whether Procrastination Is Making Your Life Better Or Bitter.

In the previous step, you have established why procrastination has stuck to you like a tick. Now, thanks to your beloved habit, your life is the way it is. Do you love the kind of life you are living right now and the achievements you have made this far? Are you proud of it? Can you say that it is the best you would have done or do you suspect that you have the potential to do better?

For instance, if you aspired to become a successful blogger and 2 years down the line, have done nothing substantial to fulfill this goal, who or what do you have to blame? A month ago, you embarked on organizing and decluttering your house but have not accomplished this goal. You have been waiting for the perfect time when you are free and relaxed. You want to lose weight but you are yet to start working on your fitness regimen – there are parties everywhere and you have not had a chance to clean your diet.

The truth is none of the reasons you give yourself are true; they are just mere excuses. The real culprit and the main reason why you are still overweight, your house is still full of clutter and that blog has never seen the light of day, is nothing but your bad habit of procrastinating things.

Now think of the kind of life you can live and enjoy if you worked on overcoming this bad habit and actually worked on your goals. You could complete your projects on time, finish off one high priority task after another and increase your productivity, spend time with loved ones, have time to spare to work on your passions and other goals – you could get to write that blog. You would also feel relaxed, organized and focused.

Compare the two scenarios. Which one would you prefer? I bet you would like the second one better – anyone would love to live such a life. Now, do you see how better things would be if you kicked the procrastination habit to the curb? This should encourage you to have better thoughts and feelings about working as hard as you can to get things done. Working should no longer be the barrier that prevents you from having a good time and working on things you love. It should now be the only way you get to do those things and also have time to enjoy your life. This way, procrastination should not be as attractive.

3: Build an Intention to Improve

You want a better life and now you are sure that you will not get it if you continue entertaining the procrastination habit – it has to go. Now it's time to build an intention to eliminate this problem from your life for good. This helps you set a commitment that reminds you of your goal whenever you go astray or feel like quitting – because changing a negative habit such as this is not easy.

To build this intention, say, "I procrastinate but I am working at improving it." Write this suggestion a few times and speak it as you write; it will help to embed this in your mind. When you speak it, do so with full conviction so you can convince your mind to believe it. Remind yourself of your intention before going to bed and after waking up every day – it should be like lullaby and your wake up song.

4: Seek To Find Meaning In Your Work

You now know why you procrastinate, have established that it is indeed making your life bitter. Since you want a better life, you have built an intention to improve. It is safe to say that you are moving in the right direction. However, you have this one more thing that you need to do if you do not want to find yourself going back to that bad habit; find meaning/value in your work. This will be enough to push you to get out of your comfort zone and set your mind and body to get into action. How do you do this? Here are some tips:

Think of future consequences and benefits in the present

The human brain is more inclined on the short-term because it likes instant gratification. Many times, you will work on something to gain benefits set in the future. For instance, you are supposed to study hard for four years or more to graduate with a college degree or work hard at challenging tasks to get a wage at the end of week or month.

Also, some consequences are set to occur in the future. For example, you had a plan to start writing a book in the beginning of the year but you have put it off promising to start next month. You will think that you have a chance to write that book until you find yourself without a page to show in the last month and that's when you realize that you failed yourself.

The best thing is:

Bring future consequences of procrastinating and future benefits of action into the present. Here are a few suggestions on how you can do that:

- **Set deadlines**: Usually, tasks have a set deadline. For instance, you may have a full year to finish your thesis – this seems like you have so much time and that's how you may end up procrastinating until the last minute. You do not have to rely on the main deadline; you can set closer deadlines of your own. For instance, give yourself a week to do all the research you need on a particular field, then set another deadline for when you are supposed to collect all the information you gathered together and put it in an organized format. This way, you are able to get a lot more work done – because the rewards are closer.

- **Break big tasks into smaller manageable pieces**: Small pieces are easier to start and manage compared to wholesome tasks that appear tiring – the reason why they are easily put off. Also, these pieces are finished quickly and thus they provide more immediate rewards.

- **Reward yourself for small wins**: you do not have to wait for the end of a mega task to reward yourself. You can have small rewards for the small wins to keep you going until the ultimate win where you get the big reward. For instance, you can go out for a drink you love, say a milkshake, every time you finish writing about one field included in your thesis as you wait for the two day vacation reward after completing it.

Remind yourself of the benefits of abstract concepts

Four years or more for a college degree may seem pointless. How do you spend so much time and money only to be handed a piece of paper? Why not spend these resources to start a business that could yield millions within the same period? This is how a person procrastinating on starting on their degree is likely to think.

Education is one among the abstract concepts. It may not give you satisfaction here and now and it may seem like you are investing too much only to get too little. However, there will come a time when that piece of paper will prove too valuable – there will be an opportunity and that paper will be your ticket. For this reason, when it comes to working for it, do not view it as the paper it is. Motivate yourself to work hard by viewing it as a ticket to a higher status.

Appreciate the many benefits that you get from working

Sometimes things get hard with the tasks that we have to do. We hate our jobs, chores and responsibilities. When this kind of negativity sets in, we result in the comfort of procrastination. What if you decided to counter it?

Think of how your work helps you live a better life and all the ways it helps you accomplish your life goals. No matter how much we dread working, work, irrespective of its type, benefits us in one way or another. If the work lacked benefits, we would not be doing it in the first place.

Whether it is doing laundry or making your marketing plan, both tasks offer you some benefits. When you think of them, you will learn to appreciate your work more. Also, you will be motivated to keep at it. For instance, if you have to work on creating your own blog but have been postponing the task, think of the benefits you will get by having a blog. It will give you recognition, it will help you curve an identity, you can use the blog to publish your work under your own name and there you can express yourself freely about areas you are passionate about. Also, it will help you get and connect with your followers.

An easy way of reminding yourself of the benefits is by jotting them down in your journal. Whenever you feel so much negativity about work that you can barely lift a finger to act, refer to this journal and remind yourself of the good getting in action brings to you.

Work less

In the world we are living in today, most of us are trapped in a rut of work, work and more work. Apparently, more work means that you earn more. This is why it may be absurd if anyone were to tell you to work less. However, did you know that overworking can throw your life off balance and compromise your creativity? Check this out.

When you allocate too much of your time to work, there will be none or too little left for your friends, family and other interests that are important to you. These are people and things you need so that you can have a balanced life. You may argue that you have to work to make a living – which is true. However, working takes care of a part of your life while the other is neglected. Eventually, you will end up with stress and anxiety. No one can work well like this; they will either be busy but not effective, engaging in tasks that are not worth the time putting off important tasks or doing work carelessly all of which lowers productivity.

You will be helping your work if you work less. How?

You are able to take care of all parts of your life. You will have time to spend with family, friends and commit to other interests outside of work. This way, you will be less anxious and stressed about life. For instance, if you spend the weekend playing a sport you love or on a family outing, you will be more relaxed and psyched to start work on Monday compared to if you spend this time grinding on work.

So, how do you work less in this fast paced world?

- Do not be that person who pulls all the work to themselves believing that only they can do it well. Train and learn to trust others whom you can delegate work that you do not need to do yourself to.

- Do the work that matters; stop engaging in tasks that are not worth your time.

- Determine your values and priorities. Include work and determine where it falls on that list.

Lower your expectations for comfort

Most of us go through life looking for comfort; we have an incessant desire to be comfortable. However, life is not comfortable always. It is full of hard stuff and sometimes it will be unfair. If you expect that things will be easy all the time, you will be disappointed.

Work is a part of life. Sometimes things will be smooth, other times they will get incredibly hard; therefore, you should set your expectations accordingly if you want a smooth sail. Expect the difficulties and when they come, instead of complaining, take this as an opportunity to step back and learn. This way, you will not dread work when things get hard. You will learn to love it for better or worse.

Live in line with your values

No matter how much you try to appreciate your work, you will be struggling to work at it every single day if it does not fit in with your values. You see, anything that you engage in that does not reflect what your values i.e. what you believe in, will be emotionally, mentally, spiritually and even physically challenging. This will lead to aversion, which is automatically a procrastination technique. In this case, when procrastination occurs, it is simply telling you that you ought to be doing something else that you believe in.

It is very important that whatever you do is in line with your value. Unfortunately, most of us have no idea what those are and we may keep struggling at a task, becoming chronic procrastinators. Here are a few ideas on how to find what aligns with your values;

- With a pen and paper in hand, evaluate yourself and write down the characteristics of a life that you would say is ideal.

- Write down a list of behavioral traits that you aspire to – that which you believe would make a great you.

- Pay attention/ be mindful of your reaction to your actions. The way you react will tell you if you really like who you are and what you do.

- Not to suggest that you jump from one job to another but you should not stick with a job that does not work for you. You are allowed to experiment

Note: Values are probable to change over time as you grow and learn from new experiences. For instance, you may be interested adventure when you are younger but later, you want a calmer and more settled life. Your values are on an ongoing basis, so do not be afraid to reassess when they change. Remember, when you are living and working within your values, you will be excited to live every day. You will stay happy, motivated and productive. Now that you have learnt how to cure your mind from the disease of procrastination and have fixed your relationship and perception of work and procrastination, it's time to move forward towards action. Before you act, you need to plan. Let's get to the planning phase below.

Step 4: Know Your Goal and Plan Accordingly

Procrastination is likely to come in when one does not have a clear sense of direction. When you do not know where you are headed, you will go anywhere any road leads. Likewise, when you do not know which tasks you need to complete, the goal you are pursuing, and the steps you need to take to accomplish that goal, you are likely to feel overwhelmed, confused, and even lack interest. This consequently paves way for procrastination whereby you delay your work for unimaginably long periods.

To ensure you get out of this vicious cycle of procrastination, have a clear vision of what you want achieve and then plan your work accordingly beforehand so you have a clear sense of direction. Let us see how you can do that.

1: Clarify the Goal You Want to Achieve

To create an effective plan, you need to have a clear idea of your pursuit. Your goal could be anything from trying to become better at your day job to starting an online business, building a stronger bond with your kids or becoming physically fitter.

All these goals are good. However, you need to be clear on which ones you want to pursue and in which order. Actually, you should not only keep them in mind but also have them in writing. If you want be to fit, make it serious by writing it down first. This is the only way a goal moves from a want to start becoming a real part of your life.

This step is supposed to help you find out and make clear to your mind what you are trying to achieve so you can then clarify the direction in which you want to steer your life. Remember, you can have different goals for different aspects of your life.

When setting goals, keep in mind that sometimes priorities, preferences, and interests change and you begin to yearn for something different. Revisiting your goals helps you set meaningful and valuable goals you truly want to fulfill. When you are working to achieve things that are meaningful to you now, you will be more enthusiastic about their pursuit.

2: Create Your Action Plan

Once you have clarity on your goal, create an action plan. An action plan charts a way that you will follow to achieve your goal so you know how to move forward.

The first step when making an action plan is to find out the time frame in which you can complete the work needed. To do so, first analyze this goal so you can understand how long it shall take you to accomplish it. To actualize your goal, will you need a year or more? If your goal spreads across a year, break it down into a smaller milestones you can achieve in 6 months which can contribute to the achievement of the bigger goal. You could then chop that 6-month goal into 2 smaller goals each taking a period of 3 months to achieve.

Keep chopping each of your smaller goals into milestones you can achieve on a weekly and then daily basis. This will make them easier to work on.

For instance, if you wish to run your own drop shipping business from an investment of $5,000, and you wish to break-even in a year, your 6 month goal could be to have recovered at least 50% of your initial investment. Your 3 month goal could be to have more visitors visiting your website. Your monthly goal could be to direct money into advertising so you can target more people, your weekly goal could to be to increase awareness of your business amongst your target market, and your daily goals could be to communicate with vendors, take orders, update your website, etc.

The good thing about having daily goals is that they give you something concerning your ultimate goal to do daily so that instead of staying idle, you do something empowering and valuable. This helps you stay focused on the goal and to constantly add value, which helps you actualize your long-term goals.

The next step is to assemble all your daily and weekly tasks and goals and arrange them in an orderly manner whereby one the accomplishment of one directly leads you to the other. When you do this, you will have before you a clear plan of action.

To increase clarity, write it down. Put on paper the steps you need to take in a chronological order. Beside each step, write in detail how you intend to execute a certain step. For instance, if one of your tasks is to find more vendors for your drop-shipping business, write down a few strategies that shall help you do that. This not only helps you to stay focused but it also makes the work easier to do. It also gives you a sense of direction, and leaves you with no reason to procrastinate.

NOTE: If, to fulfill your goal, there are skills you have to improve or shortcomings you need to overcome, include them in your action plan. For instance, if your goal is to become a web developer but you are not good at coding, add 'improve my coding skills' to your action plan and then find effective ways to accomplish this. In most cases, procrastination develops when you feel you lack enough potential or skill to do a certain task successfully. However, if you improve your skill/potential and become good enough, you will not have anything to complain about or any reason to resort to procrastination.

3: Do Not Forget to Prioritize

While working on your plan, do not forget to prioritize your work. Prioritizing your work means differentiating an important task that can increase your productivity from an unimportant one that will not have an impact on your success. Make sure you complete one or two high priority tasks every day which are crucial to the achievement of your goal. This ensures that you do something important that gets you closer to your goal every day.

To discern between a high priority and a low priority task, ask yourself this, "How will this affect my productivity, and "Will this help me achieve my goal?" For instance, if your goal is to lose 10 pounds and you are thinking about exercising or going grocery shopping, ask yourself which task will help you achieve this goal. Naturally, exercising will help you lose weight fast and therefore, this is your high priority task.

4: Plan Ahead

Once your plan of action is ready, do not hide it in your closet. Instead, go through it every night before sleeping and make necessary changes according to the situations and experiences you encounter – which sometimes vary. This helps you plan for the next day so you wake up and jump straight into action instead of wasting valuable time in the morning when you are supposed to be on the peak of your productivity, thinking of where to start.

Let's assume that according to your action plan, you should prospect for investors on Thursday but a certain contingency you faced on Wednesday demands that you deal with a client on Thursday. If you plan for Thursday on Wednesday night, you will update your action plan for the next day beforehand. This will ensure that you allocate time for the original tasks for that day and also find an appropriate time to fit in the new event such that nothing is neglected and there is no pressure.

The planning phase is only but the beginning of a task- it just helps you draw a clear path towards your goal. You can make a lot of plans but there is only one thing that matters in the long run – actualizing them with action. So, once you are through with the planning, it is time to work on the plan you created and get stuff done for real. The following step tells you how to do that.

Step 5: Take Real, Meaningful Action

Nothing works well without a plan. However, action crowns it. If you fail to work on your plan, all the planning in the world shall prove naught; you will never get to start or complete the tasks it takes to fulfill your goals. To supercharge your success, you have to take action.

Now, let's be real. If you have been caught up in inaction; you have befriended procrastination for far too long, taking action will not be easy for you. Worry not; the strategies below can help you overcome this problem too.

1: Do a Task Right Away

One of the most effective ways to get stuff done fast is to employ immediate action. Do a task the moment you assign it to yourself or the moment someone assigns it to you. Neil Patel, the co-founder of Kiss Metrics and Crazy Egg swears by this hack. According to him, when you postpone a task, you never GSD (get shit done) and work starts piling up.

To do your work on time, attend to a chore the minute you think of doing it. If you are supposed to send an email to a potential investor, do it right away. If you need to prepare a meal for dinner, prepare it right now. When you go through your daily action plan each morning, instantly attend to the first task (a high priority task) so you become charged.

Employ the 5 second rule

Mel Robbins is famous for the TEDx talk about the 5 second rule. According to her, it takes five seconds for an impulse to wear out. For instance when you feel like you should do something, say start on a book, approach a potential client or speak up to give your opinion in a meeting, all of which could open doors for you, do it immediately. Count down from 5 to 1 then jump to action. Ms. Robbins advices that you should not wait for more than 5 seconds because that is when the mind, which is used to running on autopilot applies emergency brakes, then the discouraging voices jump in to deter you. That's when you start to question if people will like your opinion or doubting if you are well prepared and just like that, the self-saboteur wins – you never get to act. To counter this, once you get the impulse to do something count back from 5 then start regardless of how unsure you feel.

When you apply the above techniques, you will see that once you complete one task successfully, you will feel motivated and energetic enough to tackle the next one.

2: Do it for 2 Minutes

If the urge to procrastinate instead of working overwhelms you, trick yourself into believing you shall work on a task for 2 minutes and no more. According to Thanh Phan, the managing director of Asian Efficiency, this '2 minute hack' works like a charm.

To practice it, just tell yourself "I will do this task (name of task) for 2 minutes only" and then get started. When you allow yourself to do something for as little as 2 minutes and then end it, you easily trick your mind to begin working on that task – the difficult part which causes many to procrastinate is to just get started. What usually happens is that once you get started on the task, you shall have started to build momentum which keeps you going long after the lapse of the 2 minutes.

Practice the 2 minute hack frequently and you will find yourself getting more stuff done. Continue challenging yourself by increasing the duration to 5, 10, and 15 minutes and then an hour. How effective this task is at helping you beat procrastination shall amaze you. Soon enough, starting on a task even when you know it will take three hours will no longer be a struggle.

3: Meditate for 2 Minutes

According to Tony Stubblebine, meditating daily is a great way to increase your focus on tasks, take action, and beat procrastination. How?

We often feel lazy and resort to procrastination because we are not living in the present moment. When we cannot focus on what we should be doing and improving our present, we easily give in to our urge to procrastinate. For instance, you may be working on an article but you are thinking about your friend's wedding tomorrow. Do you think you will get the article done? You will most likely produce substandard work or postpone it when you realize you have lost your mojo and time is far much gone.

It is evident that lack of concentration in the present moment and the task at hand keeps us from taking meaningful action daily and moving closer to our goals. To keep this from happening, make meditation a daily practice.

Why meditation?

Meditation is a wonderful practice that improves your state of mindfulness, and the ability to live in the present so you can acknowledge it, and make the most of it. Naturally, when you are consciously aware of your present, you stay focused on what you ought to be doing right now, and instead of spending your time distracted or building castles in the sky and end up postponing a task or napping, you work on it. Tony Stubblebine meditates daily so he can bring his awareness to the present and focus better on his work. This has helped him overcome the urge to procrastinate every time he feels the urge to get lazy and do so.

While there are many ways to meditate, here is a quick and easy practice for you.

1. Sit somewhere quiet and close your eyes. If you are in a noisy room, go into the bathroom or somewhere that affords you 2 minutes of quiet.

2. Before you close your eyes, set a 2-minute timer on your phone or watch.

3. Trying to breathe as naturally as possible, take a deep breath in. Focus on your breath as it enters your nostrils and goes all the way to your lungs, refreshing every cell. Focus on how it makes you feel.

4. If you feel a sensation at any part of the body, observe it and stay with your breath throughout your meditation session. Staying with your breath means you observe it as you inhale and as you exhale.

5. Every time you find yourself thinking of something else, say, "This thought can wait" and gently return your attention to your breath. However, do not force the thought out as this is likely to interfere with your concentration; acknowledge it and let it pass without paying attention to it. Count your breaths in your head to stay mindful of them.

6. Do this for 2 minutes and when your timer beeps, open your eyes very mindfully; let them open slowly and naturally.

At the end of this practice, you will feel a lot more relaxed, focused, and mindful. Now think of what you ought to do right now and start working on it immediately. Transfer the mindfulness you gained from the practice above to your task; let your mind stick to the task at hand and if any distracting thought appears; let it pass without focusing on it. This will ensure you stay focused on the task and can keep your attention and thoughts from drifting off to other things.

Meditate every day before getting started on your daily action plan and eventually start doing it before every task. You will be amazed at how quickly your focus and consequently your productivity improve.

4: Try the Pomodoro Technique

Michael Sliwinski, the CEO and founder of Productive! Magazine and Nozbe is a big believer in the Pomodoro Technique and always uses it whenever he needs to overcome procrastination. The Pomodoro Technique is an effective time management hack created by Francesco Cirillo. Cirillo used a tomato shaped kitchen timer to complete his work and since the Italian name for a tomato is 'Pomodoro,' he named the technique 'Pomodoro.'

How does it work?

In this technique, you first have to decide which task you want to complete. The second step is to break it into smaller tasks of about 3 to 4 work intervals of 25 minutes each separated by tiny breaks. Once you have settled on the task and set the work intervals, start working on it right away. You are required to analyze each work interval after its completion. This helps you learn from your mistakes in each interval, improve on them, and complete subsequent work faster. Every time you find yourself steering towards procrastination, break that task into smaller work intervals; this will get you into a work rhythm that murders procrastination especially that which happens when we feel overwhelmed by the size of work.

5: Focus on the Bigger Picture

According to Charlie Gilkey, the founder of Productive Flourishing, the procrastination monster is most likely to strike when you take your eyes off the bigger picture: your end goal. Whenever he feels the urge to procrastinate, he goes deeper into the whys of a project. He shifts focus from the when's and hows and instead focuses on why he decided to do it in the first place. This helps him retrain his focus on the bigger picture and use it as an impetus to get his bum back on track.

Likewise, each time you feel the urge to procrastinate a task, take out the list of benefits a task and how achieving it will make your life go through it a few times. By doing this, you will be reminding yourself why you started. When your why is strong, the how and laziness does not matter. You will get into action.

6: Trick Yourself with a Reward

Rewards and treats are magical: they can lure you into doing something when all you want to do is put it off. To ensure you work on your daily goals, set a nice reward you can enjoy at the end of the day after completing all the chores scheduled for that day. For instance, if your plan says you do complete 3 high priority tasks and you complete all of them, you could take yourself (and a friend) for a movie date, order a pizza at home, or do anything else that makes you happy.

7: Do Your Scariest Task First

While the advice to do your most difficult task first thing in the morning may seem controversial, this hack is one of the most effective 'overcoming procrastination hacks' there is.

Called 'eating an ugly frog in the morning' this hack dictates that you should complete a big, difficult, and scary task first and probably save the easy ones for last.

Jeff Sanders, a well-known public speaker and author swears by this hack and always practices it whenever he feels the urge to procrastinate. According to Jeff, whenever he has a difficult task scheduled for the day, he does it first even before exercising and doing other things in his morning routine. This ensures he does not burn out the energy and motivation needed to do it such that he ends up putting it off. Because he 'eats an ugly frog first,' he skyrockets his productivity.

The good thing about doing a task that scares you first is that it starts you off confident and with a high level of motivation. It feels like you killed a monster which scared you out of your wits. Now you are sure that if you killed that one, the others will be easy. You will match through your day, not afraid of the tasks lined up with an 'I have the power to handle just about anything' attitude. With the biggest task done, you are less likely to fear handling the smaller ones.

To move towards your goals smoothly, implement these super-amazing hacks each time you have to work on task on your action plan. Remember to journal how you did a task, the problems you experienced while doing it, and how you tackled these problems. This helps you track your performance and better understand and improve your strengths and weaknesses.

Conclusion

We have come to the end of the book. Thank you for reading and congratulations for reading until the end.

All of us have the ability to do great things. However, it is only by becoming committed to what we want and beating procrastination that we can actually achieve success. I hope this book has given you the knowledge you need to accomplish that goal and build a meaningful life.

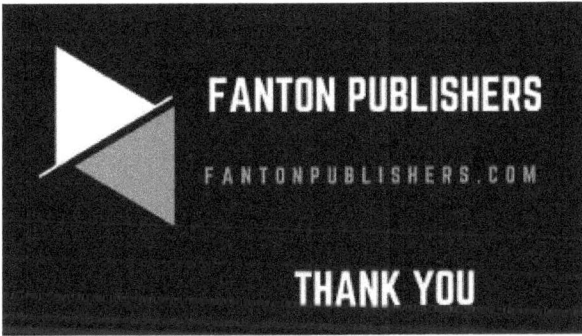

FANTON PUBLISHERS

FANTONPUBLISHERS.COM

THANK YOU

If you found the book valuable, can you recommend it to others? One way to do that is to post a review on Amazon.

Please post a review for this book on Amazon!

Thank you and good luck!

Do You Like My Book & Approach To Publishing?

If you like my writing and style and would love the ease of learning literally everything you can get your hands on from Fantonpublishers.com, I'd really need you to do me either of the following favors.

1: First, I'd Love It If You Leave a Review of This Book on Amazon.

2: Grab Some Freebies On Your Way Out; Giving Is Receiving, Right?

I gave you a complimentary book at the start of the book. If you are still interested, grab it here.

5 Pillar Life Transformation Checklist: http://bit.ly/2fantonfreebie

3: Check Out My Other Books On Productivity

Habit Building: How To Build Good Habits to Transform Your Life and Create Lasting Change without Feeling Overwhelmed and Frustrated

PSS: Let Me Also Help You Save Some Money!

If you are a heavy reader, have you considered subscribing to Kindle Unlimited? You can read this and millions of other books for just $9.99 a month)! You can check it out by searching for Kindle Unlimited on Amazon!

www.ingramcontent.com/pod-product-compliance
Lightning Source LLC
Chambersburg PA
CBHW031134020426
42333CB00012B/378